CECIL COUNTY
PUBLIC LIBARY
Ave.

D1311995

For Stefanie Von Borstel, who keeps my list growing —J. W.

To my mom, Zoe, and her garden of
plants and words —S. G.

Text copyright © 2017 by Jennifer Ward • Illustrations copyright © 2017 by Susie Ghahremani
All rights reserved. No part of this book may be reproduced or transmitted in any form or by any means, electronic or mechanical,
including photocopying, recording, or by any information storage and retrieval system, without permission in writing from the publisher.

First published in the United States of America in February 2017 by Bloomsbury Children's Books
www.bloomsbury.com

Bloomsbury is a registered trademark of Bloomsbury Publishing Plc

For information about permission to reproduce selections from this book, write to
Permissions, Bloomsbury Children's Books, 1385 Broadway, New York, New York 10018
Bloomsbury books may be purchased for business or promotional use. For information on bulk purchases
please contact Macmillan Corporate and Premium Sales Department at specialmarkets@macmillan.com

Library of Congress Cataloging-in-Publication Data
Names: Ward, Jennifer, author. | Ghahremani, Susie, illustrator.
Title: What will grow? / by Jennifer Ward ; illustrated by Susie Ghahremani.
Description: New York : Bloomsbury Children's Books, 2017.
Identifiers: LCCN 2016016126 (print) • LCCN 2016031717 (e-book)
ISBN 978-1-68119-030-3 (hardcover) • ISBN 978-1-68119-031-0 (e-book) • ISBN 978-1-68119-032-7 (e-PDF)
Subjects: LCSH: Plants—Reproduction—Juvenile literature. | Seeds—Juvenile literature. | BISAC: JUVENILE NONFICTION / Science & Nature /
Flowers & Plants. | JUVENILE NONFICTION / Science & Nature / Environmental Science & Ecosystems. | JUVENILE NONFICTION / Concepts / Seasons.
Classification: LCC QK825 .W37 2017 (print) | LCC QK825 (e-book) | DDC 575.6/8—dc23
LC record available at https://lccn.loc.gov/2016016126

Art created with gouache on wood • Hand-lettering by Susie Ghahremani; typeset in Cronos Pro • Book design by Susie Ghahremani
Printed in China by Leo Paper Products, Heshan, Guangdong
2 4 6 8 10 9 7 5 3

All papers used by Bloomsbury Publishing, Inc., are natural, recyclable products
made from wood grown in well-managed forests. The manufacturing processes
conform to the environmental regulations of the country of origin.

WHAT WILL GROW?

JENNIFER WARD

illustrated by **SUSIE GHAHREMANI**

BLOOMSBURY

NEW YORK LONDON OXFORD NEW DELHI SYDNEY

PEAS.

WHAT
WILL
GROW?

LETTUCE.

SHINY, BROWN.
BUMPY CROWN.

WHAT WILL GROW?

OAK TREE.

DANDELION.

VERY TINY.
THEN SO VINY!

WHAT WILL GROW?

TOMATO.

STRIPY BLACK.
CRUNCHY SNACK.

WHAT WILL GROW?

MILKWEED.

APPLE TREE.

PUMPKIN.

RADISH.

SNUG, TIGHT.
PAPER LIGHT.

WHAT WILL GROW?

SEEDS!

Each plant creates its own seeds, and inside every seed is a plant that wants to grow. Seeds come in many shapes and sizes. You can plant a seed indoors in a pot, or outside in the ground, and watch it grow. The seeds below require soil, water, and sunshine.

ACORN (OAK TREE SEED)

SOW: Fall

STEPS: Gather acorns and remove the caps; soak acorns in water overnight, then discard the ones that float; bury acorns in soil about 1 inch deep, providing plenty of space for growth

WHEN WILL IT GROW? In the spring, a *sapling* (baby tree) will sprout, maturing to a shade tree in about 20 years

CARROT SEED

SOW: Early spring

STEPS: Bury ½ inch deep in loose soil free of rocks, spacing 4 inches apart

WHEN WILL IT GROW? Matures in about 90 days

LETTUCE SEED

SOW: Early spring

STEPS: Sow indoors in pots, using a pencil tip to create a small hole for each seed; after a few weeks, transplant to your outdoor garden, planting in rows

WHEN WILL IT GROW? Matures in about 30 days

APPLE SEED

SOW: Fall

STEPS: Bury seeds 1 inch deep where there is room for each to grow; cover with a light layer of soil and then with sand

WHEN WILL IT GROW? Sprouts in the spring; matures in about 6 years

DANDELION SEED

SOW: Spring

STEPS: Bury just below surface of soil

WHEN WILL IT GROW? Matures in 80 to 90 days

MILKWEED SEED

SOW: Fall

STEPS: Bury ¼ inch deep or scatter on loose soil in a sunny area

WHEN WILL IT GROW? Sprouts in the spring; blooms in the summer

PEA SEED

SOW: Early spring

STEPS: Bury in loose soil 1 inch deep, about 4 inches apart; provide trellis for plant to climb

WHEN WILL IT GROW? Matures in about 60 days

PINE TREE SEED

SOW: Fall

STEPS: Gather seeds from closed pinecones; soak seeds in water, keeping only those that sink; plant in pots indoors, pointy side down; transplant outdoors in the spring

WHEN WILL IT GROW? Most pine trees grow 1–2 feet per year

PUMPKIN SEED

SOW: Late spring or early summer

STEPS: Bury 1 inch deep and at least 4 feet apart

WHEN WILL IT GROW? Matures in about 100 days

RADISH SEED

SOW: Late summer for winter radishes

STEPS: Bury seeds in a sunny space ½ inch deep in loose soil free from rocks, 3 inches apart

WHEN WILL IT GROW? Matures in about 35 days

SUNFLOWER SEED

SOW: Spring

STEPS: Bury 1 inch deep and 6 inches apart

WHEN WILL IT GROW? Matures in about 70 days

TOMATO SEED

SOW: Late winter to early spring

STEPS: Begin in a pot indoors; bury ¼ inch deep; transfer to outdoor garden once flowers are present; provide trellis to support growing plant

WHEN WILL IT GROW? Matures in about 80 days

FROM SEED TO PLANT

STAGE 1: ROOTS

Roots are the first thing to grow from a seed. They hold the plant in the soil and take in water.

STAGE 2: STEM

A stem grows. The stem helps the plant stand up and moves water from the roots to the rest of the plant.

STAGE 3: LEAVES

The leaves soak up sun to make food for the plant.

1.   2.   3.

STAGE 4: FLOWER

The flower or fruit—depending on the plant—produces seeds, and then the cycle begins again!